D1207063

Oprah
Winfrey

Read These Other
Ferguson Career Biographies

Maya Angelou
Author and
Documentary Filmmaker
by Lucia Raatma

Leonard Bernstein
Composer and Conductor
by Jean F. Blashfield

Shirley Temple Black
Actor and Diplomat
by Jean F. Blashfield

George Bush
Business Executive
and U.S. President
by Robert Green

Bill Gates
Computer Programmer
and Entrepreneur
by Lucia Raatma

John Glenn
Astronaut and U.S. Senator
by Robert Green

Martin Luther King Jr.
Minister and
Civil Rights Activist
by Brendan January

Charles Lindbergh
Pilot
by Lucia Raatma

Sandra Day O'Connor
Lawyer and
Supreme Court Justice
by Jean Kinney Williams

Wilma Rudolph
Athlete and Educator
by Alice K. Flanagan

Oprah Winfrey

Entertainer, Producer, and Businesswoman

LUCIA RAATMA

Ferguson Publishing Company
Chicago, Illinois

Photographs ©: Mitchell Gerber/Corbis, cover, 52; Evan Agostini/Liaison Agency, 8, 81; Steve Green/AP/Wide World Photos, 10; Reuters/Fred Prouser/Archive Photos, 12; Metropolitan Archives, Nashville/Davidson County, 17, 32, 34; AP/Wide World Photos, 18, 37, 39, 41, 65, 73; Frank Driggs Collection/Archive Photos, 25; Don Perdue/Liaison Agency, 28; Faverty/Liaison Agency, 43; Barry King/Liaison Agency, 46; Bettmann/Corbis, 48; Hulton Getty/Harcourt Brace/Liaison Agency, 53; Archive Photos, 55; James Schnepf/Liaison Agency, 57; Reuters/Brad Rickerby/Archive Photos, 60; Tom Gates/Archive Photos, 62; Capital Cities/ABC/Archive Photos, 64; Reuters/Jeff Christensen/Corbis, 69; Victor Malafronte/Archive Photos, 71, 94; Chris Kasson/AP/Wide World Photos, 74; Fotos International/Archive Photos, 79; Arnaldo Magnani/Liaison Agency, 84; George Burns/AP/Wide World Photos, 86; Bettmann/Reuters/Gary Cameron/Corbis, 89; Robert Mulherin/Liaison Agency, 91; AFP/ Tannen Maury/Corbis, 98.

An Editorial Directions Book

Library of Congress Cataloging-in-Publication Data
Raatma, Lucia.
    Oprah Winfrey / by Lucia Raatma.
    p. cm.—(Ferguson career biographies)
    Includes bibliographical references and index.
    ISBN 0-89434-376-9
    1. Winfrey, Oprah—Juvenile literature. 2. Television personalities—United States Biography—Juvenile literature. 3. Motion picture actors and actresses—United States—Biography—Juvenile literature. [1. Winfrey, Oprah. 2. Television personalities. 3. Actors and actresses. 4. Afro-Americans—Biography. 5. Women—Biography.] I. Title. II. Ferguson's career biographies.
PN1992.4.W56 R33 2001
791.45′028′092—dc21
[B]   00-048396

Copyright © 2001 by Ferguson Publishing Company
Published and distributed by
Ferguson Publishing Company
200 West Jackson Street, Suite 700
Chicago, Illinois 60606
www.fergpubco.com

Printed in the United States of America
Y-3

CONTENTS

Oprah
Winfrey

Woman of words. Over the years, people around the world have listened to Oprah.

A STRONG VOICE

When Oprah Winfrey walks onstage each day to tape her talk show, the audience cheers. When the show is aired on television, people all over the world watch. Oprah has a powerful presence, and nearly everyone wants to hear what she has to say. She has a remarkable influence on people of all ages and from all backgrounds. As writer Fran Lebowitz once said, "Oprah is probably the greatest media influence on the adult population. She is almost a religion."

What is amazing about Oprah is the route

she took to get where she is now. She is not the daughter of a movie star or the cousin of a well-known director. Instead, she is the daughter of a poor, unmarried woman from the rural South. Oprah's childhood was a difficult one, and she had a

Talking with Hillary Rodham Clinton. Oprah's guests are often prominent people in our culture.

number of homes—but Oprah believes that these difficulties made her the woman she is today. She is quick to explain, "I don't think of myself as a poor deprived ghetto girl who made good. I think of myself as somebody who from an early age knew I was responsible for myself, and I had to make good."

Oprah's career began in the radio business but she has since gained many other skills. Today, she is a famous talk-show host, actor, producer, activist, and magazine publisher. Throughout her life, Oprah has taken chances. Sometimes she has failed, but mostly, she has succeeded. And her success has improved the lives of people all over the world.

Years of changes. Oprah has come a long way from her difficult childhood.

HARD BEGINNINGS

Oprah Gail Winfrey was born on January 29, 1954, in Kosciusko, Mississippi. Her name was supposed to have been Orpah, a name from the Bible's Book of Ruth. From the very beginning, however, there was confusion about her name. Her birth certificate reads "Orpah," but most people did not know how to pronounce it. They reversed two of the letters, creating the name "Oprah."

Oprah's mother, Vernita Lee, did not marry Oprah's father, Vernon Winfrey. After Oprah was born, Vernita had very little to do with her daughter. In fact, she soon moved to Milwaukee, Wisconsin, leaving Oprah on the farm in Kosciusko with her grandparents, Hattie Mae and Henry "Earless" Lee.

Life on the Farm

Oprah's grandparents did not have much money. They grew food to eat and sold chicken eggs for extra income. Oprah's clothes were all made by her grandmother, not bought in stores. The family had no plumbing, so instead of a bathroom, they had an outhouse. They had to bring buckets of drinking water into the house from a well. Oprah was usually barefoot. She wore shoes only for church on Sunday.

Earless Lee was a frightening man, and Oprah was terrified of him. She remembers, "I feared him. Always a dark presence. I remember him always throwing things at me or trying to shoo me away with his cane." Oprah felt very loved by her grandmother, however, and even called her "Momma." Nevertheless, Hattie Mae was a strict disciplinarian. As a little girl, Oprah often received several whippings a week, even for slight misbehavior. Today, Oprah feels that such treatment would be considered child abuse.

Despite this harsh treatment, Oprah always felt close to her grandmother. Some of Oprah's earliest memories are of sitting on the front porch with her grandmother and attending the Faith-United Mississippi Baptist Church with her. At as early as age three, Oprah often recited Bible passages in front of everyone at church. These experiences were her introduction to being onstage and performing.

Oprah credits her grandmother for making her into the woman she is today. She says that she learned strength and a sense of reasoning from Hattie Mae. She remembers her childhood as a lonely one, however: "The nearest neighbor was a blind man up the road. There weren't other kids . . . no playmates, no toys except for one corncob doll. I played with the animals and made speeches to the cows."

"I Do Not Think I Belong Here"

Even as a little girl, Oprah was very smart. In addition to memorizing Bible verses, she also learned to read at an early age. So when she entered kindergarten, she was bored. She wanted to do more than draw and play. She wrote a note to her teacher: "Dear Miss New," it read, "I do not think I belong here."

Miss New saw how bright Oprah was and agreed with her. Oprah skipped kindergarten and went directly to first grade. The next year, she skipped second grade too.

No matter how smart Oprah was, she was still a little girl and adults made most of the decisions in her life. When Oprah was six years old, everything changed. She left the farm life she had always known and went to join her mother in Milwaukee, Wisconsin. Vernita had decided that she now wanted to live with her daughter as a family. Vernita had a boyfriend who promised to marry her, and they had a daughter named Patricia. Patricia was Oprah's half-sister.

Living in Milwaukee was very hard for Oprah. She was used to living on the farm and spending all her time outdoors. In Milwaukee, she lived in a rooming house. The city was noisy and crowded. Vernita worked long hours as a maid, and the family did not have much money.

A New Home

After two years, the family's home life had not improved. Vernita's boyfriend did not marry her after all, and Vernita was having a hard time supporting her two daughters. She asked Vernon Winfrey if Oprah could live with him in Nashville, Tennessee. Vernon and his wife, Zelma, had no children, so they were happy to have Oprah join them.

The time Oprah spent with her father and stepmother was good for her. They expected a lot from her, and she liked the structure and discipline they enforced. They were not as harsh as Hattie Mae had

Vernon Winfrey. Oprah's father tried hard to make his daughter's life a good one.

been, and they gave Oprah love and respect. Even in the summer months, Oprah had work to do. Oprah remembers, "My stepmother was real tough, a real strong disciplinarian, and I owe a lot to her because it was like military school there. I had to do book reports at home as well as in school and so many vocabulary words a week." Zelma also drilled Oprah on the multiplication tables.

Oprah enjoyed the attention she got from Vernon and Zelma. She studied hard at school and made good grades. She had a number of friends, and she continued to give performances at church.

Nashville in 1965. Oprah learned a lot from her father and stepmother while she lived with them.

Leaving Again

After a year in Nashville, Oprah's life changed again. Vernita had a new boyfriend and another baby, Jeffrey. She wanted to try to make her family life work again, so she asked Vernon if she could have Oprah back.

Oprah did not want to leave her father and step-mother, but her mother begged her. At first, Oprah thought she was going to Milwaukee for just one summer, but her mother refused to let her go back to Nashville. Oprah lived there in a two-bedroom apartment with her mother, her mother's boyfriend, Patricia, and Jeffrey.

Oprah learned that having a sister could be difficult. She learned that African-Americans were often treated differently from white people. And she learned that being smart is not always a good thing.

She remembers: "I felt really ugly in this environment because I believed that the lighter your complexion, the prettier you were. My new sister was lighter and she got all the attention, and I thought it was because she was the prettiest. I was the smartest, but no one praised me for being smart. I was teased because I was sitting in a corner reading; people made fun of me for that. And I felt really sad and left out. My books were my only friends."

Oprah and her mother did not have a close relationship. Oprah wanted a life like those she saw on television. She was jealous of the families on *Leave It to Beaver* and *I Love Lucy*—and she was disappointed with her own family. She wanted hugs and encouragement, but she did not get them. She remembers that Vernita "was tired. And she was just trying to survive. Her way of showing love to me was getting out and going to work every day, putting clothes on my back and having food on the table. At that time I didn't understand it."

Loss of Innocence

Oprah's imperfect family was not the only problem she faced as a child. When she was nine years old, she had a terrifying and sad experience. While Vernita worked, Oprah was often left with an older male cousin. Although Oprah never felt comfortable around him, she had to stay with him. She had no choice. One night, the cousin raped her. Oprah had no idea what was happening—but she knew it was wrong and she knew it hurt very badly.

The cousin later took her to the zoo and bought her ice cream. He told her that she could never tell anyone what he had done, or they would both be in trouble. Oprah believed what he said and kept the attack a secret. She has still never revealed the man's name.

Unfortunately, Oprah experienced more sexual abuse. She was raped in her own house by men who were visiting her family. She was even molested by her favorite uncle. Oprah kept all these attacks secret. She was afraid her family would think that being raped was her fault. She even began to wonder about that herself. She wondered if she were somehow to blame for the actions of these men—which, of course, she was not.

These terrible crimes have had a deep effect on Oprah throughout her life. She explains, "What it does to you, you cannot come out of it without being touched in some way. What it did for me is that it made me a sexually promiscuous [unrestrained] teenager. And it's very confusing, because if it's the first time in your life anyone has ever shown you any kind of affection or attention, you confuse that with love, and so you go searching for it in other places."

Books and Other Friends

While facing all these problems at home, Oprah always had a refuge—a place to turn. She turned to books. Reading took Oprah away from all that was happening to her, even if only for a little while. She explains, "Books showed me there were possibilities in life, that there were actually people like me living in a world I could not only aspire to but attain. Reading gave me hope. For me, it was the open door."

Oprah excelled in school and loved the attention she got from her teachers. When she was in the fourth grade, she remembers, "Something came over me. I turned in a book report early and it got such a good response, I thought, 'I'm gonna do that again.'" Throughout her adult life, Oprah has praised her teachers for all they did for her. She has singled out Mary Duncan, her fourth-grade teacher, for helping her to believe in herself.

She also has kind words for Eugene Abrams, the teacher who helped her get into Upward Bound, a program that helped low-income students prepare for college. Oprah says, "For every one of us [who] succeeds, it's because there was somebody out there to show you the way out. The light doesn't necessarily have to be your family; for me it was teachers and school."

For the Upward Bound program, Oprah had to travel each day to Nicolet High School, which was located in a Milwaukee suburb. She had to wake up very early and take three buses to get to the school. The effort was worthwhile, however. In this learning program, Oprah was more challenged than she had ever been before.

Troubles

Although she had academic success, Oprah's personal struggles continued. She was the only African-American student at Nicolet High School. The other students were friendly to her but treated her as if she were different from them. They would invite her to their homes—but would then introduce her to their servants. They would ask her if she knew Sammy Davis Jr., a black entertainer who was popular at that time. They had the strange idea that all African-Americans knew one another because they shared a skin color. Visiting these homes, Oprah realized just how poor she and her family really were. She was embarrassed and often made up stories about herself to impress her new friends.

After a while, Oprah started staying out late and stealing money from her mother. She wanted to fit in and to be liked by the other students. Soon she became sexually active with a number of boys. She was looking for love and attention but, unfortunately, she was going about it in the wrong way.

Oprah began acting out her frustrations and fears in other ways too. She once wanted expensive designer eyeglasses, but her mother told her they could not afford them. Oprah was angry and, one day, when she was home alone, she broke her plain, inexpensive glasses. She also threw furniture and broke other objects. When she stopped and realized what she had done, she decided to lie about her actions. She called the police and told them that the apartment had been robbed. The police took a report but they were not sure Oprah was telling the truth. When Vernita saw the broken glasses, she knew her daughter was lying.

Another time, Oprah went to visit friends. The friends were not at home, so Oprah just kept walking. Soon she came upon a beautiful limousine parked outside a fancy hotel. Oprah wondered what it would be like to be rich enough to have a limousine and stay in a hotel. Just then, a woman stepped out of the car. It was the famous singer Aretha Franklin. Oprah approached the singer, crying, and told her that she was lost and needed money. Franklin was touched by the convincing story and handed Oprah a $100 bill. Oprah used the money to stay in a cheap hotel for a week, and then went home. Vernita began to realize that her daughter had serious problems.

Aretha Franklin in the 1960s. This young singer helped Oprah when she ran away from home.

The problems become more serious when, at the age of fourteen, Oprah became pregnant. The baby was born prematurely and died soon after. This part of Oprah's life was extremely difficult. Her family was not sympathetic. They still did not know that she had been sexually abused, so they did not understand why she was involved with boys. No one talked to her about the pregnancy or about the baby she had lost. They just pretended that the whole thing had never happened.

Vernita felt that she could no longer control her daughter. She tried to have Oprah admitted to a home for troubled teens, but the program had a two-week waiting period. Feeling that she couldn't bear even two more weeks, Vernita called Vernon Winfrey and again asked him to take Oprah back. Vernon was sad to hear about all the trouble Oprah was in, and he wanted to help. Oprah remembers, "I'm grateful to my mother for sending me away. If she hadn't, I would have taken an absolutely different path in life."

A Second Chance

When Oprah returned to Tennessee, Vernon and Zelma picked up where they had left off. Immediately, they gave Oprah's life discipline and structure. She began to work in the grocery store Vernon owned. The store was near the Faith United Baptist Church that the family attended, and many of the church members shopped there. Oprah hated working at the store, but the job taught her to have a sense of responsibility. Vernon was stern and expected a great deal from her.

Every two weeks, Zelma took Oprah to the library to get five books. Oprah had to read all the books and write reports on each one. Oprah's love of books grew. She read many books written by all kinds of authors, but two books were especially meaningful for her. One was *Jubilee* by Margaret Walker, the story of a slave whose father was her mother's master. The second book was *I Know Why the Caged Bird Sings* by Maya Angelou, about the early life of the author.

Oprah could easily relate to the story of Maya Angelou's life. Like Oprah, Angelou was also abandoned by her mother and then later lived with her for a time. Angelou was also sexually abused at a young age and had a baby when she was a teenager. Despite her early difficulties, Angelou became a talented and successful poet. Her story inspired Oprah.

Maya Angelou. Oprah was influenced by this writer's work, and later the two women became friends.

In fact, Oprah believes that Angelou must have been her mother in another life. Today, the two women are close friends.

While Oprah was living with Vernon and Zelma, she was expected to study hard. She was allowed to watch only one hour of television a day—the local and national news. Vernon told his daughter that there were three different kinds of people in the world: "There are those who make things happen.

There are those who watch things happen, and there are those who don't know what's happening." He expected his daughter to be the kind of person who makes things happen.

A Rising Star

In the late 1960s, many schools were becoming integrated—which meant that black and white students attended the same schools for the first time. Until then, blacks and whites had been required to attend separate schools. The integration of schools was an important part of the civil rights movement of that period. Many people disagreed with integration, however. Some white people still believed that black people should remain separate.

Oprah entered East High School in Nashville, Tennessee, when the idea of integration was quite new. She was treated badly by some white students who resented her being there. This was one of the first times that Oprah had encountered racism firsthand. At first she was upset and angry, but then she decided to try and change things. She performed readings from books by important African-American authors. She did oral reports on slavery fighters, such as Harriet Tubman and Sojourner Truth.

Many students were impressed by Oprah's words, and they began to listen to her. Oprah joined the school debate team and the drama club. She was even elected president of the student council.

With the help of teachers and family members, Oprah had turned her life around. At age sixteen, she was named as a representative to a youth conference in Colorado, which was sponsored by the White House. Oprah traveled to Los Angeles with another youth group. While in Hollywood, she visited the famous Grauman's (now Mann's) Chinese Theater. She stared at all the handprints and footprints that famous entertainers had left in the cement blocks of the sidewalk. Oprah rubbed her hands along the names written in the bronze stars of the Hollywood Walk of Fame and vowed that, one day, she would have a star there too.

MAKING NEWS

I n her senior year, Oprah was named the most popular girl at East High School. Her boyfriend, Anthony Otey, who was also an honor student, was named the most popular boy. Together, they served on a number of committees and did volunteer work in the community too. They even helped raise money for the March of Dimes by participating in a walkathon.

In a walkathon, each participant asks sponsors to donate a certain amount of money for every mile the person walks. One of Oprah's sponsors was WVOL, a local radio

Miss Fire Prevention. In 1971, Oprah won this title and her life began to turn around.

station. When Oprah went to the station to collect the donation, she met a disc jockey named John Heidelberg. He was immediately impressed with the way Oprah spoke, so he asked her if she'd like to read the news. At first, she thought he was kidding, but he convinced her to make a demo tape that day. He later played the tape for his station manager. Suddenly, seventeen-year-old Oprah was offered a part-time job after school and on weekends—reading the news on the radio.

Vernon Winfrey was not sure if he approved of his daughter's working at the radio station. He worried that people there would take advantage of her. He also felt Oprah should concentrate on her schoolwork. But Oprah begged him to let her take the job. She promised not to date anyone from the station, and she insisted that she would keep up her grades. Finally, her father agreed.

After an initial training period, Oprah was making $100 a week. She was excited to be making an income. The job also taught her a great deal about current events in Nashville, Tennessee. Soon Oprah began to gain more confidence. She thrived in the exciting atmosphere of the radio station.

On Stage Again

The annual Miss Fire Prevention contest was a tradition in Nashville. This beauty pageant was sponsored by the fire department, and many local businesses chose employees to be contestants. Although the past winners had always been white, WVOL asked Oprah to represent the station in the 1971 pageant.

On stage. Oprah gained confidence in beauty pageants, and soon she was ready to pursue a journalism career.

During the pageant, each contestant was asked what she wanted to do with her life. Many said they wanted to raise families or become teachers. Oprah had often considered becoming a fourth-grade teacher because she so admired her own fourth-grade teacher, Mrs. Duncan. When she was asked the question, she suddenly remembered watching journalist Barbara Walters on the *Today* show. Oprah answered, "I believe in truth. And I want to perpetuate the truth. So I want to be a journalist."

Oprah impressed the judges, and she became

one of three finalists. The last question for the young women was: What would you do if you had a million dollars? The first woman said she would help her family. The second said she would help the poor. Oprah said, "If I had a million dollars, I'd be a spending fool!" The judges were so surprised by her honesty that Oprah won the contest.

The next year, Oprah was in three more beauty contests. Oprah won the first contest, Miss Black Nashville, and received a four-year scholarship to Tennessee State University. She was thrilled at the thought of a scholarship, but she was disappointed too. She had always hoped to go away to college, not to a school that was only 7 miles (11.3 kilometers) from home.

During the Miss Black Tennessee contest, Oprah again impressed the judges with her poise and her speaking skills. She won that crown, too, and would next head to Hollywood for the Miss Black America pageant.

But Oprah was beginning to have doubts about these beauty contests. She wanted to do so many things with her life, and she wasn't sure that winning another crown was one of them. During the Miss Black America pageant, she didn't follow her adviser's suggestions for dresses and hairstyles. Oprah was not chosen as a finalist, but she didn't seem upset at all. She kissed the winner and said good-bye to the friends she had made. Some people believe that she lost the national contest on purpose.

On Campus

The 1970s were a difficult time at Tennessee State University. The mostly African-American student body joined much of black America in its discontent with the civil rights movement. Many felt that the movement had not helped the African-American people. They felt that the efforts of Martin Luther King Jr. and Malcolm X had not accomplished enough. Some students believed that African-Americans should take over the U.S. government. Some wanted to create an all-black country. Others wanted to return to Africa.

Oprah did not agree with any of these ideas, however. She had never felt that the color of her skin had kept her from doing anything she wanted to do. She also firmly believed that blacks and whites needed to respect one another and work together. Oprah had heard the civil rights leader Jesse Jackson speak. She chose to follow his advice. "He said

Jesse Jackson in 1973. His words helped Oprah come to terms with the unfairness she saw in the world.

that excellence is the best deterrent to racism and sexism, that the greatest contribution you can make to women's rights, to civil rights, is to be the absolute damnedest best at what you do."

So Oprah concentrated on her classes. She decided to major in drama and performed in plays on campus. She also continued to work at WVOL. Oprah had no desire to march in demonstrations with the other students, so many of them disliked her. Overall, Oprah found college to be a disappointing experience.

On Television

When Oprah was still a sophomore in college, she heard of an opening at WTVF, the CBS television station in Nashville. At first, she wasn't sure if she should apply for the job. She was worried that the responsibilities would interfere with her schoolwork. Her drama professor encouraged her to try.

When she arrived at the television station, Oprah realized she did not know how to act in front of a camera. So, she decided to imitate the *Today* show host she admired. "I had no idea what to do or say. And I thought in my head that maybe I'll just pretend I'm Barbara Walters. I will hold my head like Barbara. So I crossed my legs at the ankles, and I put my little finger under my chin, and I leaned across the desk, and I pretended to be Barbara Walters." Her technique worked, and Oprah was offered the job.

During this time, many businesses were under pressure to hire minority employees. Oprah knew the station was pleased that she represented two minority groups: She was a woman and an African-American. Oprah did not hesitate to take advantage

Barbara Walters in the 1970s. Oprah admired this journalist and hoped to one day be like her.

of the station's needs. She remembers, "Sure I was a token, but honey, I was one happy token."

Because Oprah was still in college, she was still living at home. Vernon worried that this new job would interfere with Oprah's studies. However, when he found out that she was being paid $15,000 a year—the same salary he made—he knew he couldn't argue. He had already learned that Oprah had a mind of her own.

Part of her job was to be the weekend news anchor, and the other part was reporting stories throughout Nashville. She enjoyed the anchor position, and she had an easy presence in front of the camera. She found the work as a reporter more difficult. She could do the reporting, but the stories were often sad. Oprah was strongly affected by news about crime and tragedy. It was hard for her to hide her emotions and keep a professional distance.

On to Baltimore

When Oprah was a senior in college, she received another exciting job offer. WJZ, an ABC television station in Baltimore, Maryland, asked her to be a reporter and a co-anchor for the evening news. If she moved to Baltimore, Oprah would not be able to finish her senior year in college—but she could not pass up this opportunity. Her father was disappointed that she didn't graduate, but Oprah was excited about what her future would hold.

Baltimore is a bigger city than Nashville, and

In the big city. Oprah moved to Baltimore for a job at WJZ television.

Oprah's salary was higher. She was eager to be out on her own, living away from her family for the first time. By this time, Barbara Walters, who had been with the *Today* show, was anchoring the ABC evening news with Harry Reasoner. She was reported to be making $1 million a year. So Oprah set a goal for herself—to be a millionaire by age thirty-two.

Doing It Her Way

Oprah approached her new job with enthusiasm, but some people worried about her style. When anchoring, she didn't like to read the news ahead of time, so sometimes she mispronounced words on camera. She laughed when she made mistakes, and she often spoke without following the prepared script.

Oprah also continued to have trouble reporting. At the scene of a fire, for example, she would be in tears as she reported the details. Seeing people in such trouble was heartbreaking for Oprah, and she could not control her emotions. After eight months, the management at WJZ began to have doubts about whether she was suited to reporting. Oprah admitted that she might not be cut out for hard news.

The station had signed a long-term contract with Oprah, however, so they had to find another position for her. First, they sent her to a salon for a makeover—which turned out to be a big mistake. The hairdresser used a permanent solution that made all Oprah's hair fall out! For months, she had to wear scarves while her hair grew back. Next, the station sent her for speech lessons. There was actually nothing wrong with the way she spoke. In fact, she had often been praised for her diction and for the fact that she spoke without any accent. The speech coach just told her to toughen up and fight for her rights.

The Right Path

In 1977, a new station manager arrived at WJZ with an idea for a new show. Since 1967, Phil Donahue had been the host of a successful talk show. Donahue's style was unique. He carried his microphone into the audience so that people could speak for themselves. Today, this type of talk show is very

Phil Donahue and his viewers. Donahue was the first talk-show host to take his microphone into the audience.

common, but Phil Donahue was the first to develop it. Donahue's show was based in Chicago but was broadcast all over the country.

Because *Donahue* was so successful, WJZ's station manager decided to start a talk show too. He called it *People Are Talking*. The show would be hosted by two people. The male host was Richard Sher, and Oprah was chosen to be the female host.

Many people thought the show would fail, and Oprah thought she was given the job so the station could get rid of her. But the program was a hit. Oprah remembered, "The minute the first show was over, I thought 'Thank God, I've found what I was meant to do.' It's like breathing to me."

People Are Talking beat Donahue in the Baltimore television ratings. Soon, the show was picked up by twelve other cities across the country. Oprah was becoming a well-known television star.

Personal Problems

Although Oprah was succeeding professionally, her personal life was difficult. She had always had a hard time with relationships. Often, she would grow so attached to the man she was dating that she began to believe she could not live without him. Her lack of confidence was probably caused by the abuse she had experienced as a child.

Oprah had dated a man in Baltimore for four years, but the relationship had not worked out. After they broke up, she felt very sad and lonely. She remembers, "I had so much going for me, but I still thought I was nothing without a man. . . . The more he rejected me, the more I wanted him. I felt depleted, powerless. Once I stayed in bed for three days . . . I just couldn't get up." Slowly, she was able to overcome her neediness. She learned to rely on herself instead of others for her sense of self-worth.

A Best Friend

During Oprah's time in Baltimore, she met Gayle King. King was a production assistant at the television station. Oprah explains how their friendship began: "One night, there was a terrible snowstorm, so I invited Gayle, who was then living about thirty-five miles away, to stay at my house. She did—and we sat up and talked until dawn! Ever since then, we talk every day, sometimes three or four times."

Even though Oprah and Gayle now live in different parts of the country, their close friendship remains. They have often worked together too. In

Special friends. Gayle King got to know Oprah in Baltimore, and the two have been close ever since.

fact, Gayle is now editor-at-large of *O, The Oprah Magazine.* About Oprah, Gayle says, "She was there when I got married and she was there when I got divorced and she was there when my children were born. We're very, very close. And I'm absolutely nuts about her."

CENTER STAGE

With the success of *People Are Talking,* Oprah was getting noticed. She was also getting restless. She wanted to move on, perhaps to a bigger city. At the same time, Debbie DiMaio, an associate producer of the show, decided to do something new too. She began sending out tapes of *People Are Talking,* hoping to get a job as a producer somewhere.

Dennis Swanson viewed one of the tapes. He was the general manager of a show called *A.M. Chicago* in Chicago, Illinois. Swanson was impressed by DiMaio's work,

Oprah in 1986. She achieved great success after her move to Chicago.

but he also liked what he saw in Oprah. He recalls, "Never had I seen anything like Oprah. . . . So spontaneous and unrehearsed. She was not like anyone else on [television]." Before long, DiMaio was hired to produce *A.M. Chicago*. By the end of 1983, Oprah was hired as its new host.

A.M. Chicago

When Oprah first thought about moving to Chicago, she was worried. A new city would mean new offices, new friends, and lots of new experiences. Also, the show *Donahue* was based in Chicago, and it aired at the same time as *A.M. Chicago.* Many people wondered if Oprah's show could compete with Phil Donahue's. Oprah had become much more confident in the past several years. She decided it was time to prove herself—and *A.M. Chicago* gave her a great chance to do that.

Oprah had the support of her friend Gayle King. King told her, "Leave Baltimore! I know you can beat Donahue!" To this day, Oprah insists it was the best advice Gayle ever gave her.

Despite her worries, Oprah loved Chicago. She remembers, "I set foot in this city and just walking down the street, it was like roots, like the motherland. I knew I belonged here." The Chicago audience immediately loved Oprah too. *A.M. Chicago* was a big hit, and it beat *Donahue* in the ratings.

At the time, Oprah said, "I like Phil Donahue, but I have to admit it feels good to beat him. For the longest time, I couldn't go about doing my job without people saying, 'Yeah, you're good. But are you as good as Donahue?'" Oprah has always had great respect for Phil Donahue. She knows that he improved the quality of daytime talk shows and that she benefited from the work he did.

Struggling with Stress

Even though Oprah was good at her job, she was often scared that the show would fail. One of the ways that Oprah dealt with her stress and worry was by eating. As many people do, Oprah found comfort in food.

Unfortunately, this habit caused her to gain a lot of weight. Oprah was already heavy when she arrived in Chicago but quickly put on another 20 pounds (9 kilograms). She remembers, "I thought I was handling the stress just fine. The show was going well. I was doing great. Everyone told me how easy I made it all look. But underneath I was terrified. So at night I'd sit up all alone in my room at the Knickerbocker Hotel and order French onion soup by the gallon. . . ." In the years to come, Oprah would continue to struggle with her eating habits.

The Secret of Success

Within twelve weeks, *A.M. Chicago* had more viewers than *Donahue.* After seven months, Oprah's half-hour show was extended to an hour. Oprah and her producers planned many different topics for the shows. She interviewed celebrities, such as singer Paul McCartney and actors Goldie Hawn, Sally Field, and Candace Bergen. She also did programs about weight loss, different types of abuse, and various personal problems. Oprah even interviewed members of the Ku Klux Klan, a group of people who believe whites are superior to all other races. Although Oprah was troubled by this group's ideas, she tried to present them in an honest way. This direct and open approach is one of the reasons for her great popularity.

Producer Debbie DiMaio explained Oprah's secret of success: "She's 100 percent the same off-camera as on. People like her because they can relate to her. She's got all the same problems—overweight, boyfriend troubles, she's been poor. So when people see her on television they can say, 'That's my friend Oprah.'"

Two other challenging interviews for Oprah were those with Barbara Walters and Maya Angelou. She credits both women for inspiring her. Oprah so admired these women that she was nervous about speaking with them. She found it hard to find the

With Barbara Walters. Oprah found interviewing her role models to be exciting yet emotional.

right words when she was on camera with them. Despite Oprah's nervousness, however, both interviews were heartfelt and sincere.

The Color Purple

One of Oprah's favorite books has always been *The Color Purple* by Alice Walker. This novel won a Pulitzer Prize in 1983. The story is about a black woman who is abused by men but who learns to live independently. Oprah read the book in 1982 and started to give copies to friends for any occasion. When she heard that *The Color Purple* was being made into a film, she wanted to work on it in some way. Little did she know then that she would actually star in it.

The musician Quincy Jones was one of the producers of the film. While he was visiting Chicago, he watched Oprah's show on the television set in his hotel room. He was impressed by her and thought she would be great in the role of Sofia, one of the

Alice Walker. One of her books, The Color Purple, *had long been a favorite of Oprah's.*

movie's main characters. Jones contacted Oprah and set up an audition.

When the film's director, Steven Spielberg, saw Oprah's audition tape, he asked her to come in for another audition in person. He agreed with Jones that she was the right choice. Oprah was cast in the role of Sofia. She loved the character. Sofia is a strong woman who overcomes her husband's abuse and even survives time in jail. Through it all, Sofia keeps her strength and dignity. Some of Sofia's lines described feelings that Oprah herself may have had about her own life: "All my life I had to fight. I had to fight my daddy, I had to fight my uncles, I had to fight my brothers. A child ain't safe in a family of mens."

Some people complained because Steven Speilberg, who is white, was directing the film. They did not believe that he could understand the black experience well enough to create the movie. Oprah found Spielberg to be an intelligent and sensitive director, however. She learned a great deal from him and from the other actors, including Danny Glover and Whoopi Goldberg.

When *The Color Purple* hit the theaters, audiences were moved by the powerful story. Some

On screen. Oprah gained praise for her performance as Sofia in The Color Purple.

movie critics, however, were not impressed. Some of them said that the film presented black men in a bad light. Others felt that the dialogue was not realistic. Oprah was quick to defend the film. "It's about endurance, survival, faith, and ultimate triumph," she said.

A Night at the Oscars

Although the film had been criticized by some, it received eleven Academy Award nominations. Oprah was nominated in the category of best supporting actress. Her performance also led to her nomination for a Golden Globe Award.

Everyone who had worked on *The Color Purple* looked forward to Oscar night. Steven Spielberg, known only for blockbuster films at that time, wondered if he would win his first Oscar. Oprah also looked forward to an exciting night. The evening was a disappointment, however. *The Color Purple* did not receive a single award. Oprah was actually relieved that she didn't win. The dress she was wearing was too tight. She had been uncomfortable all night and worried about having to walk up to the stage. But Oprah had enjoyed her first acting experience—and she had many more ahead of her.

The Oprah Winfrey Show

In 1985, Oprah received some good advice from her attorney. He suggested that if she wanted to keep control of her television show, she should own it. That way, she could rent the show to various television stations, but it would always be hers. This renting-out process is called syndication. Oprah took her attorney's advice—and made history. She purchased *A.M. Chicago* and renamed it *The Oprah Winfrey*

With Jeffrey Jacobs. This entertainment lawyer has helped Oprah make her show what it is today.

Show. She became the first woman to own and produce her own talk show.

A Country Full of Fans

People across the United States had seen Oprah perform in *The Color Purple,* but her TV show aired only in Chicago. After buying the rights to the talk show, Oprah and her staff began working on its syndication. They teamed up with King World Productions, a company that syndicated *Jeopardy* and *Wheel of Fortune.* For months, tapes of Oprah's show were sent to television stations in various cities throughout the country. Oprah even visited many of them in person.

All these efforts paid off. On September 8, 1986, *The Oprah Winfrey Show* made its first appearance as a national program. Some people didn't like Oprah's style, and others disliked the way she looked. But most of the viewers thought she was great.

People throughout the country were now able to tune in to hear what Oprah had to say. They loved listening to her interviews with her interesting guests. They appreciated her honesty and sense of humor. The television stations made millions of dollars by selling advertising that would air during her show. By the end of 1986, Oprah made an estimated annual income of $30 million. She had met her goal of becoming a thirty-two-year-old millionaire—and then some.

A Very Good Year

Oprah had other reasons to be happy, too. In 1986, she starred in another film, *Native Son.* The script was based on a novel by the acclaimed African-

American writer Richard Wright. Although the movie did not do well in the theaters, Oprah was praised for her performance.

She was thrilled by the experiences she had while making this film and was inspired to make more. She founded her own production company, Harpo Entertainment Group. ("Harpo" is "Oprah" spelled backward.) Harpo Entertainment Group has several divisions: Harpo Productions, Inc., Harpo Films, and Harpo Video, Inc. With this new project, Oprah made history again. She became one of only three women ever to own their own production companies. The others were silent-film star Mary Pickford and comedian Lucille Ball.

Another reason for Oprah to be happy was personal. She had met a man named Stedman Graham. Stedman is a former model and basketball player. In 1986, he was running a program called Athletes Against Drugs, and he often met Oprah at parties and other events in Chicago. He asked Oprah on dates many times before she finally agreed to go out with him. After their first dinner together, she knew she had found a good relationship. She remembers, "He bought me flowers, paid for dinner, and was interested in what I had to say!" At last, Oprah was

Always a couple. Stedman Graham and Oprah began dating in 1986.

receiving the respect and admiration she had longed for from a man.

Graduation

In 1986, Oprah also decided she had some business to finish up. She had left Tennessee State University before graduating so that she could take the job at WJZ in Baltimore. Oprah was always unhappy that she did not receive her degree. Her father had urged her to finish and he, too, was upset that she had not. Oprah finally contacted the university and arranged to take part in a project that would earn her a degree.

Oprah received her bachelor's degree the next year. She not only attended the graduation, but the school also asked her to be the guest speaker. She felt privileged to address the other graduates. In her speech, she praised her father for all his support. That day, she started the Vernon Winfrey Scholarship Fund. Each year, Oprah selects ten students to receive scholarships named in honor of her father.

Emmy Awards

Each year, the Academy of Television Arts and Sciences gives awards for the best shows on television. The awards are called Emmys. They are given to programs in each of several categories. The Daytime Emmys are awarded to soap operas, talk shows, and game shows. In 1987, Oprah won the first of the many Emmys she would receive. She won the award for best talk-show host. *The Oprah Winfrey Show* won the award for best talk show.

Award winner. Oprah won her first of many Emmys in 1987.

Oprah had come a long way from her early life in Mississippi. She had overcome many problems and met many challenges. She had developed self-confidence and created a successful career and personal life. Through hard work and determination, she had become one of the best in her field.

EVERYBODY'S GIRLFRIEND

A FEW YEARS AFTER the national syndication of her show, "Oprah" had become a household word. Celebrities were eager to appear on her show. Authors hoped for a chance to talk with her on camera and promote their books.

Women viewers, especially, are drawn to Oprah. Many consider her an understanding friend, even if they never meet her in person. Oprah listens closely to people and offers helpful advice for solving everyday problems. Most of all, people feel she is "human" and just like everyone else. Even

A good listener. Oprah's friendly style helps her guests to open up and be themselves.

Oprah is amazed by how warmly she is received by the public: "People out there think that I'm their girlfriend; they treat me like that. It's really amazing."

Oprah Winfrey: Entertainer, Producer, and Businesswoman

With Michael Jordan. Oprah has interviewed sports stars and other celebrities, as well as everyday people.

Sharing Secrets

For years, Oprah had never told anyone about the sexual abuse she had experienced as a child. She may have been ashamed of what happened. Or she may still have been blaming herself—even though she was older and should have known otherwise.

In 1985, Oprah finally told her secret. She didn't plan to—it just happened. A guest on her show was talking about being raped by members of her own family. The people in the audience were very touched by the story. Women were calling in to say that they, too, had been victims of sexual abuse. Oprah remembers, "The guest I was interviewing started crying, and I started crying and told for the first time that it had happened to me too."

Some critics have accused Oprah of telling her secret that day just to gain ratings, but most believe that she spoke from her heart. Once again, Oprah admitted that she had problems just like everyone else did. That fact only made her audience feel closer to her. After the show, Oprah realized, "I no longer had to live with the horrible secret, and I knew it could help others who had suffered the same way."

Oprah's honesty has, in fact, helped many people. Since that show, women from all backgrounds have been able to talk about the abuse they have experienced. Oprah's show brought the subject of sexual abuse into the open. Her discussions have since helped teachers, police, and others to recognize the signs of sexual abuse in children and adults.

Weight Control

Many people worry about the way they look, and Oprah is no different. When she was in beauty pageants in the early 1970s, she weighed 135 pounds

(61.2 kg). Although she was fairly slender, she always had to watch what she ate. As she got older, however, she often turned to food when she was feeling stressed or upset.

When Oprah was living in Baltimore, she weighed about 150 pounds (68 kg). Convinced that she needed to be thinner, she tried many different diets. All these programs worked for a while—but every time she went off a diet, she gained more weight. Oprah explains, "I didn't realize at the time that by overeating I was trying to fill something deeper. The fact that I was lonely, somewhat depressed, and having a hard time adjusting to the new job never entered my mind." By the time she moved to Chicago, Oprah weighed 172 pounds (78 kg).

The stress of her new television show caused her to gain even more weight. She was soon up to 180 pounds (81.7 kg). A few years later, while attending a boxing match, Oprah was shocked to find out that she weighed as much as Mike Tyson, a heavyweight fighter. She had reached 216 pounds (98 kg). She continually tried to diet, but never had any real success.

Shortly after that, Oprah heard of a liquid diet called Optifast. She was determined to make that diet work. She set herself goal—to fit into a pair of size 10 jeans. Oprah stayed on the liquid diet for four months. She ate no solid food at all.

On November 15, 1988, Oprah proudly wore the size 10 jeans on her show. And she came onstage pulling a red wagon. The wagon held almost 70 pounds (31.8 kg) of animal fat sealed in plastic. Oprah wanted to show her audience just how much body fat she had lost. She now weighed 142 pounds (64.5 kg).

Unfortunately, once again, her success did not last. Within a year after she started eating solid food again, Oprah was back up to 168 pounds (76.3 kg). Before long, she weighed 200 pounds (90.7 kg), and she was angry with herself.

In 1991, Oprah visited a health and beauty spa in southern California. There she met Rosie Daley, the spa's chef. Oprah was enthusiastic about all the delicious, low-fat recipes that Rosie prepared. She hired Rosie as her personal cook—but still Oprah continued to gain weight. The following year, she reached her all-time high of 237 pounds (107.6 kg).

Oprah was disappointed in herself. When she attended the 1992 Emmy Awards ceremony, she was embarrassed by how she looked. She later wrote, "I felt so much like a loser, like I'd lost control of my

At the 1992 Emmy Awards. Oprah was disappointed with the amount of weight she had regained.

life. And the weight was symbolic of how out-of-control I was. I was the fattest woman in the room."

Making the Connection

At that time, Oprah did not understand that her weight problem was about more than just food. The problem had its roots in her emotions and her feelings about herself. Many people believe that the sexual abuse Oprah suffered as a child was a factor in her weight problem. Some believed that the extra weight was like a shield, protecting Oprah from those who might hurt her.

Oprah decided to spend three weeks at a Colorado spa, and things began to change. She met Bob Greene, a fitness trainer. He helped Oprah see that she needed to have a healthier lifestyle, not just worry about her weight. He encouraged her to exercise and to eat more fruits and vegetables. Oprah began walking for exercise, then moved on to running. Within eight months, she was down to 150 pounds (68 kg). In 1995, Oprah proudly ran a 26-mile (42-km) Marine Corps Marathon.

Oprah continued to get help from Rosie Daley too. In 1994, she published *In the Kitchen with Rosie,* which became a best-selling cookbook. Two years later, she and Bob Greene published *Make the Connection: Ten Steps to a Better Body and a Better Life.* That book and the videotape that followed were also best-sellers.

To this day, Oprah continues to struggle with her weight. At times, she still turns to food when she is upset. Most often, however, she remembers what Bob Greene taught her about the connection between her physical self and her spiritual self:

Oprah Winfrey: Entertainer, Producer, and Businesswoman

Getting healthy. Oprah spoke to the crowd before a run in New York's Central Park.

"That means looking after yourself every day and putting forth your best effort to love yourself enough to do what's best for you."

Talking about Men

Oprah is always willing to talk to women about men. She has lived through some bad relationships and now has a good relationship with Stedman Graham. She understands the kinds of problems many people have in their personal lives.

Because of her past experiences, Oprah always encourages women to get away from men that hurt them. She once told a guest, "You just pack your car and move out on him, you hear me?" She also advises teenage girls to get their education first, then worry about getting married or starting a family.

Some people wonder why Oprah and Stedman Graham have not married, although they announced their engagement at one point. Oprah explains that neither of them is ready for marriage and they enjoy their relationship the way it is. She says, "I am in no hurry to get married. I dislike the notion of a desperate woman who wants to get married."

Oprah can easily sympathize with people who are in relationships for the wrong reasons. She helps them to look at themselves and their motives. Once, an audience member admitted that she wasn't sure why she was engaged, that she wasn't quite ready for marriage. The young woman seemed surprised to hear herself say this—and no doubt her fiancé was shocked too. Only Oprah could inspire someone to admit such a deep, personal feeling for the first time on national television.

Tuned In

Ask most people why they watch *The Oprah Winfrey Show,* and most will say they watch because they like the host. Oprah makes people feel at ease. The viewers feel as though Oprah is sitting in their living rooms, talking just to them. When Oprah discusses her weight problems or shares her previous difficulties with men, she opens herself to her audience. Even when she makes mistakes on the air, she is not judged by those who watch and love her. Every day, she reminds her audience that we are all human, and we all have things to learn and problems to overcome.

Talking to the world. Oprah is popular because she has a good way of communicating.

Many talents. As her career progressed, Oprah proved to be good behind the camera as well as in front of it.

BEHIND THE CAMERA

ALTHOUGH SHE HAD achieved great success as a talk-show host, Oprah wanted to do more. She had many ideas for new projects. She bought a block-long building in Chicago to house Harpo Productions. It cost more than $20 million to purchase and renovate the space. The building is now a state-of-the-art studio with dozens of offices, a fitness center, and three sound stages.

One of her goals was to portray African-Americans in a realistic way on television and in films. She felt that blacks were too often portrayed as either athletes or musicians. She wanted to introduce the American people to what the lives of African-Americans were really like. She explained, "Most people out there have no contact with black people ever. . . . There's a whole reality outside what most people know, where the black community functions on its own, where people own businesses, where people care about prosperity and their children and pay their taxes. The point of having your own company is that you can show that."

Television Producer

Oprah's first project as a producer was a television miniseries entitled "The Women of Brewster Place." The story was based on a novel written by Gloria Naylor about seven African-American women. Oprah, Robin Givens, and Cecily Tyson were among the actors in the program. Oprah remembers, "It was an incredible experience. I haven't done a lot of acting and I really enjoyed it. . . . Working with these women was wonderful." Audiences liked the program. It was the highest-rated miniseries of the 1988–1989 television season.

ABC was pleased with the success of "The Women of Brewster Place," so the network offered

Oprah the chance to make the story a weekly series. Oprah quickly got the project underway. However, the new series, *Brewster Place,* which debuted in 1990, was not a success. Reviewers thought the story and characters were dull, and the show was soon canceled. Oprah admitted that the timing for the series was not right. She was so excited about the opportunity that she hadn't thought through the project. She vowed to learn from her mistakes.

Since then, Oprah has produced a number of television films. In 1993, she starred in and produced *There Are No Children Here.* The movie, based on a book by Alex Kotlowitz, portrays the real-life story of a family in one of Chicago's poor neighborhoods. The project was filmed on location in the Henry Horner Homes, a public-housing project in Chicago. Oprah was touched by the people in the film and by the people living in the neighborhood. When the project was finished, she set up a scholarship fund for the local children.

Harpo Films has a long-term contract to produce movies for ABC Television. Each one is introduced as "Oprah Winfrey Presents." These projects have included *Before Women Had Wings,* based on a novel by Connie Mae Fowler; *The Wedding,* based on

Dorothy West's novel; *David and Lisa,* starring Sidney Poitier; and *Tuesdays with Morrie,* based on sportswriter Mitch Albom's best-selling book. *Tuesdays with Morrie* received an honor from the Producers Guild of America and won an Emmy for best television movie. Its two stars, Jack Lemmon and Hank Azaria, both won Emmy awards for their performances.

The Big Screen

In addition to her television work, Oprah has signed a contract to produce films for the Walt Disney Motion Pictures Group. The first of these projects was the 1998 movie *Beloved.* The film was based on a 1987 novel by Toni Morrison. Oprah starred in the movie. Her character, Sethe, is a slave who has escaped her master but lives in a house haunted by her murdered daughter's ghost. Danny Glover, one of Oprah's costars in *The Color Purple,* was also featured in the film.

Morrison writes in a beautiful, poetic way that was difficult to capture on film. Oprah put her heart into the project and remained true to Morrison's language. The movie received mixed reviews, but Oprah was proud of what she and the studio had accomplished in making it.

With Danny Glover in Beloved. *Oprah produced and starred in the 1998 film.*

In Charge

All her life, Oprah has had big ideas about what she wanted to achieve. She has great determination, and she can sometimes be a perfectionist. This strong drive is what has helped make Oprah a success— but it can be hard on the people who work for her.

Oprah's staff has a great loyalty to her. They work long hours, and some say they drink hundreds of pots of coffee a day just to keep up with her. Oprah says she tries to rule with her heart. She has a strong head for business, but she believes that people matter more than money or success. One former producer put it this way: "People adore her. They give up their lives for her. People who work [at Harpo] get divorced, put off having kids, have no outside lives. Because everything, all your time and energy, is given to Oprah."

Through the years, however, a number of her staff members have left their positions. Some say she is tough to work for. No doubt she expects a great deal from those around her. She has learned that being a boss can be very difficult. After one troublesome incident at the studio, Oprah admitted, "I used to say, 'I never went to business school, and I've never read a business book.' But now I think, maybe I should have read a few."

Oprah On-line

In 1998, Oprah brought her energy and talents to the Internet. She announced that she would join some other producers in forming Oxygen Media.

The project includes a women's cable-television network, which was launched in February 2000. The television network is linked to Oxygen's on-line services, which include *Oprah.com*, *ThriveOnline*, and *Moms Online*.

Another project is *Oprah Goes Online*, a guide designed to help women learn how to use the Internet. Oprah, Gayle King, and others offer on-line lessons and a newsletter about E-mail, software, search engines, Web shopping sources, and other

Introducing Oxygen.com. Oprah joined other women in this Internet project.

Internet services. There is even a lesson on creating your own Web page.

Awards and Honors

The Oprah Winfrey Show has won more than thirty Emmy Awards, and Oprah has won several for best talk-show host. She has been honored in many other ways too. In 1996, she received the George Foster Peabody Individual Achievement Award. That same year, she also won the Gold Medal Award from the International Radio and Television Society.

In 1997, *Newsweek* magazine named Oprah Winfrey as the most important person in books and media. In 1998, she was on *Time* magazine's list of the 100 most influential people of the twentieth century. That year she also received the Lifetime Achievement Award from the National Academy of Television Arts and Sciences.

Oprah is grateful for these awards, but she also knows that with all the attention and praise comes great responsibility. She is a role model for many people, and she realizes the powerful influence she has on others throughout the world. She hopes that her influence will always be a positive one.

CHANGES FOR THE BETTER

ACCORDING TO 1999 statistics, 22 million American viewers watch *The Oprah Winfrey Show* each week. The show also airs in 116 other countries. Clearly, what Oprah says and does affects millions of people throughout the world.

In the mid-1980s, shortly after Oprah's show went nationwide, many other talk shows began to be produced. Some copied the format that Phil Donahue and Oprah used. Other shows were less professional. The guests got into physical fights on the air, and many of the topics were in poor taste.

At the National Book Foundation awards. Oprah was honored by the group for her contributions to books and reading.

Some critics called these programs "Trash TV."

Throughout the many years she has been on the air, Oprah has always tried to make her show upbeat and positive. One of her regular guests is Dr. Phil McGraw, a psychologist who specializes in improving relationships. She also often features interesting authors and experts on fitness and nutrition. Oprah's goal is to help people improve their lives.

The Book Club

Oprah has always loved to read. She began to worry that people in the United States were losing interest in reading. She decided to share some of her favorite books with her audience. In 1996, she launched Oprah's Book Club. Each month, Oprah selects a book for her audience to read. Then the book's author appears as a guest on her show. Oprah and selected readers join the author on the air to discuss the book together.

The book club has been a huge success. All the books Oprah has chosen have become national bestsellers. People throughout the world have become interested in reading again. The American Library Association has given Oprah credit for "single-handedly expanding the size of the reading public." In 1999,

Girl talk. One episode of Oprah's Book Club was filmed at Maya Angelou's home in North Carolina.

Oprah received the 50th Anniversary Gold Medal from the National Book Foundation for her contribution to reading and books. She has become one of the most influential people in the book-publishing world.

The Angel Network

In 1997, Oprah launched another project, called Oprah's Angel Network. The idea was simple: to encourage people to help others in need. That simple idea has since grown into a remarkable and far-reaching effort.

Some of the participants in the Angel Network have fixed up playgrounds for younger children. Some have served as baby-sitters at YMCAs while teenagers take parenting classes. Others have collected money for numerous causes.

Since it began, the network has raised $3.5 million for college scholarships. It has also helped Habitat for Humanity build more than 200 homes for people who needed them. In 2000, the network began giving the Use Your Life award. Every Monday, an award of $100,000 is given to a person who is using his or her life to help others.

Protecting Children

When a four-year-old girl in Chicago was sexually attacked and murdered, Oprah recalled her own childhood experiences. She decided to try to address the problem of child abuse in the United States. With the help of Attorney James Thompson (governor of Illinois from 1977 to 1991), Oprah drafted a proposal for a new law. This law would create a national database containing the names of people convicted of child abuse. Oprah asked Senator Joseph Biden of Delaware to sponsor her proposal in Congress.

In 1991, Oprah testified before a U.S. Senate committee to support the proposal. She talked about her own abuse and about the little girl who had been killed. In 1993, President Bill Clinton signed the new bill into law. It was known as the National Child Protection Act. Today, the database is managed by the Federal Bureau of Investigation (FBI). Schools and other groups can access the information to check the backgrounds of job applicants and employees.

In 1995, Oprah also started a year-long campaign called Child Alert. This program urged people to turn in their guns. Oprah believes that too many kids are hurt or killed by guns, and that the people of the United States, as a whole, own too many weapons.

Through the years, Oprah has often worked directly with young people. She participated in a little sister program in Chicago's Cabrini-Green housing development. She took girls from this housing project shopping, to movies, and to dinner. She talked to them about school and about boys. She even helped the girls get library cards. She explained to them what she thought they needed to succeed in life.

Making it law. Oprah and James Thompson watched as President Clinton signed the National Child Protection Act in 1993.

Speaking Her Mind

One of Oprah's best traits is her honesty. Seldom do people have to wonder what she thinks—she never hesitates to state her opinions. But, one time in particular, her honesty led to a lot of trouble.

In 1996, Oprah was doing a show about mad cow disease. This disease was being spread by cows in England. People who caught the disease by eating the affected beef experienced brain damage and, sometimes, death. As Oprah listened to an expert describe the disease, she was horrified. She exclaimed, "It has just stopped me cold from eating another burger!"

The studio audience certainly understood her reaction, but the people who raise cattle in Texas did not. These cattle ranchers felt that Oprah had been unfair to them. They believed that her strong opinion would discourage people from buying beef. The cattle ranchers sued Oprah for "unfair and biased coverage of the issue."

Oprah traveled to Amarillo, Texas, to appear in court. She lived in a hotel there for more than a month while taping *The Oprah Winfrey Show* in the city. This was a difficult period for her. Oprah appeared in court during the day, and then she and her staff taped the shows at night. While speaking in court, she admitted that she could have been better prepared when speaking about mad cow disease—but she insisted that she never meant to attack the beef industry.

Ultimately, the court decided that Oprah had a right to free expression, and she won the case. Oprah told the crowd outside the courthouse, "I will continue to use my voice. I believed from the begin-

Standing up for herself. Oprah was happy to talk to reporters in Texas after her court case was over.

ning this was an attempt to muzzle that voice. I come from a people who have struggled and died in order to have a voice in this country, and I refuse to be muzzled."

Not even a lawsuit can keep Oprah from speaking her mind. On her show and in her life, she has always voiced her strong opinions on a number of subjects. She supports gay people in their struggle for equal rights. She supports women who strive for independence. She respects people who work hard to be good parents, noting that they have "the toughest job in the world."

New Enterprises

In 1999, Oprah and Stedman Graham began an exciting new project. Together, they taught a course at the Kellogg Graduate School of Management at Northwestern University. The course, called "Dynamics of Leadership," taught students how to recognize and improve their leadership skills and how to develop management techniques.

In April 2000, Oprah took on another new role—magazine founder and editorial director. Working with Hearst Magazines, she launched *O, The Oprah Magazine*. This monthly publication encourages its readers to make the most of their lives. It offers celebrity interviews, articles about health and nutrition, self-help columns, and more.

In the magazine's first issue, Oprah described its purpose this way: "My hope is that this magazine will help you lead a more productive life, one in which you feel a sense of vitality, cooperation, harmony, balance and reverence within yourself and in all your encounters. That doesn't mean living a life without frustration, anxieties and disappointments. It means understanding that your choices move you forward or hold you back."

Oprah hopes that the magazine will provide her with another way to reach people. She hopes that this publication, like her show, will provide many with encouragement and inspiration.

The Spiritual Side

When she was a young girl, Oprah and her family always attended church services. She was instructed about morals and about faith in God. Through the years, Oprah's spiritual beliefs have grown and changed. Now, they are deeply connected to her own experiences, but she has built on the basic ideas that she learned as a child. She explains that "I have

Spiritual life. On her show, Oprah often devotes time to religious ideas.

Oprah Winfrey: Entertainer, Producer, and Businesswoman

church within myself. I have church walking down the street. I believe in the God force that lives inside all of us, and once you tap into that, you can do anything."

On her talk show, Oprah devotes much time to discussion of spiritual matters. She plans segments on spiritual spaces and practices. She invites guests to talk about forgiveness and karma (the idea that a person's actions in this life affect their existence in the next).

Oprah also often talks about her own spiritual journey. She once explained her daily habit: "What I do every morning is I go to my window. I watch the sun come up and I center myself and try to touch the God light I believe is in all of us. Some people call it prayer, some call it meditation; I just call it centering up. I get boundless, boundless energy from that. If there happens to be a day when I don't do it, I find myself loose, misdirected."

Giving Back to Others

Oprah's words touch millions of people each day— but she affects many people in financial ways too. She has become one of the world's richest people. She feels lucky to have attained such wealth, so she tries to share her good fortune with others. Oprah has donated money to many causes—for example, to aid abused women, to help AIDS victims, and to assist inner-city children. In addition to the scholarships she sponsors at Tennessee State University, she has given substantial donations of money to Spelman College and to Morehouse College, which have long traditions as black colleges.

Although her relationship with her family members has sometimes been difficult, Oprah has also always tried to help them. She has bought houses for her parents to relieve their financial burden, and she has helped out with other expenses too.

Oprah is known to be a tough boss, but she is also known as being very generous with her staff. She has taken her employees on shopping sprees. Once, she treated her staff to a vacation in the British Virgin Islands. She paid for a wedding for one of her producers and gave Gayle King a big check to buy a new house.

Oprah Winfrey will be the first to say that she leads a special life. She had her share of hard times, but she has learned from those times. Now she wants to share the wisdom she has gained with others. To Oprah, her work is a calling. As she says, "I feel that my show is a ministry; we just don't take up a collection. And I feel that it is a teaching tool, without preaching to people about it. That's my intent."

At the Top

For many years, *The Oprah Winfrey Show* has been regarded as the most successful talk show on television. Oprah says she will leave the show someday, but, for now, she is happy to continue as its host. She reaches people throughout the world through the show and through her many other film, television, and print projects. At times, she has asked the wrong questions and offended guests. She has also sometimes let personal problems keep her from reaching her goals. For the most part, however, Oprah has tried to improve the lives of the people she touches.

Oprah has had great success as a talk-show host, actress, and producer because she is not afraid to be herself. She is always willing to take chances to express what is true and real to her—and her fans respect and appreciate that. She once explained her

Meeting the people. President George W. Bush found appearing on The Oprah Winfrey Show *to be an important stop during his 2000 campaign.*

success this way: "The reason I communicate with all these people is because I think I'm everywoman, and I've had every malady and I've been on every diet and I've had men who have done me wrong, honey. So I related to all of that. And I'm not afraid or ashamed to say it. So whatever is happening, if I can relate to it personally, I always do."

TIMELINE

1954 Oprah Winfrey born in Kosciusko, Mississippi, on January 29; lives with her grandparents until age six

1960 Moves to Milwaukee, Wisconsin, to live with her mother

1962 Moves to Nashville, Tennessee, to live with her father and stepmother

1963 Moves back to Milwaukee to live with her mother

1968 Moves back to Nashville

1971 Named Miss Fire Prevention in Nashville; starts working at WVOL

1972 Wins Miss Black Nashville pageant and Miss Black Tennessee pageant; receives scholarship to Tennessee State University

1973 Co-anchors evening and weekend news for WTVF-TV

1976 Begins co-hosting local news at WJZ-TV in Baltimore

1977 Begins co-hosting *People Are Talking* at WJZ-TV

1984 Begins hosting *A.M. Chicago* at WLS-TV

1985 Purchases *A.M. Chicago* and renames it *The Oprah Winfrey Show;* stars in *The Color Purple*

1986 Is nominated for a Golden Globe and an Academy Award for her role in *The Color Purple; The Oprah Winfrey Show* becomes nationally syndicated; forms Harpo Productions; stars in *Native Son;* meets Stedman Graham

1987 Receives her degree from Tennessee State University; wins Daytime Emmys for best talk show and best talk-show host

1988 Stars in and produces television miniseries "The Women of Brewster Place"; renovates huge Chicago building for Harpo Productions

1990 Stars in and produces television serial *Brewster Place*

1991 Testifies about child abuse before a U.S. Senate committee; hires Rosie Daley as personal cook and nutritionist

1993 President Clinton signs the National Child Protection Act into law; Winfrey hires Bob Greene as a personal trainer; stars in and produces *There Are No Children Here*

1994 *In the Kitchen with Rosie* is published

1995 Runs in the Marine Corps Marathon in Washington, D.C.; initiates Child Alert

1996 *Make the Connection: Ten Steps to a Better Body and a Better Life* is published; begins Oprah's Book Club; is sued by Texas cattle ranchers for her comments about beef; receives the George Foster Peabody Individual Achievement Award and the International Radio and Television Society's Gold Medal Award

1997 Starts Oprah's Angel Network; stars in and produces *Before Women Had Wings;* produces the home video *Make the Connection;* is named *Newsweek* magazine's most important person in books and media

1998 Wins Texas cattle ranchers' court case; stars in and produces *Beloved;* named one of the 100 most influential people of the twentieth century by *Time* magazine; joins other producers in launching Oxygen Media, Inc.; receives a lifetime achievement award from the National Academy of Television Arts and Sciences

1999 Begins teaching with Stedman Graham at Northwestern University's J. L. Kellogg Graduate School of Management; receives the National Book Foundation's 50th Anniversary Gold Medal for the Oprah's Book Club contribution to books and authors

2000 Launches *O, The Oprah Magazine*

HOW TO
BECOME A
PRODUCER

The Job

The primary role of a producer is to organize and secure the financial backing necessary to undertake a motion picture project. The director, by contrast, creates the film from the screenplay. Despite this general distinction, the producer often takes part in creative decisions, and occasionally one person is both the producer and director. On some small projects, such as a nature or historical documentary for a public television broadcast, the producer might also be the writer and cameraman.

The job of a producer generally begins in the preproduction stage of filmmaking with the selection of a movie idea from a script, or other material. Some films are made from original screenplays, while others are adapted from books. If a book is selected, the producer must first purchase the rights from the author or his or her publishing company, and a writer must be hired to adapt the book into a screenplay format. Producers are usually inundated with scripts from writers and others who have ideas for a movie. Producers may have their own ideas for a motion picture and will hire a writer to write the screenplay. Occasionally a studio will approach a producer, typically a producer who has had many commercially or artistically successful films in the past, with a project.

After selecting a project, the producer will find a director, the technical staff, and the star actor or actors to participate in the film. Along with the script and screenwriter, these essential people are referred to as the "package." Packaging is sometimes arranged with the help of talent agencies. It is the package that the producer tries to sell to an investor to obtain the necessary funds to finance the salaries and cost of the film.

There are three common sources for financing a film: major studios, production companies, and individual investors. A small number of producers have enough money to pay for their own projects. Major studios are the largest source of money and finance most of the big budget films. Although some studios have full-time producers on staff, they hire self-employed, or *independent producers,* for many projects. Large production companies often have the capital resources to fund projects they feel will be commercially successful. On the smaller end of the scale, producers of documentary films commonly approach individual donors; foundations; art agencies of federal, state, and local governments; and even family members and churches. The National Endowment for the

Humanities and the National Endowment for the Arts are major federal benefactors of cinema.

Raising money from individual investors can occupy much of the producer's time. Fund-raising may be done on the telephone, as well as in conferences, business lunches, and even cocktail parties. The producer may also look for a distributor for the film even before the production begins.

Obtaining the necessary financing does not guarantee a film will be made. After raising the money, the producer takes the basic plan of the package and tries to work it into a developed project. The script may be rewritten several times, the full cast of actors is hired, salaries are negotiated, and logistical problems, such as the location of the filming, are worked out; on some projects it might be the director who handles these tasks, or the director may work with the producer. Most major motion film projects do not get beyond this complicated stage of development.

During the production phase, the producer tries to keep the project on schedule and the spending within the established budget. Other production tasks include the review of dailies, which are prints of the day's filming. As the head of the project, the producer is ultimately responsible for resolving all problems, including personal conflicts such as those between the director and an actor and the director and the studio. If the film is successfully completed, the producer monitors its distribution and may participate in the publicity and advertising of the film.

To accomplish the many and varied tasks that the position requires, producers hire a number of subordinates, such as associate producers, sometimes called coproducers, line producers, and production assistants. Job titles, however, vary from project to project. In general, associate producers work directly under the producer and oversee the major areas of the project, such as the budget. *Line producers* handle the day-to-day operations of the project. Production assistants may perform substantive tasks, such as reviewing scripts, but others are hired to run errands. Another title, *executive producer,* often refers to the person who puts up the money, such as a studio executive, but it is sometimes an honorary title with no functional relevance to the project.

Requirements

There is no minimum educational requirement for becoming a producer. Many producers, however, are college graduates, and many also have a business degree or other previous business experience. They must not only be talented salespeople and administrators but also have a thorough understanding of films and motion picture technology. Such understanding, of course, only comes from experience.

High School   High school courses that will be of assistance to you in your work as a producer include speech, mathematics, business, psychology, and English.

Postsecondary Training   Formal study of film, television, communications, theater, writing, English literature, or art are helpful, as the producer must have the background to know whether an idea or script is worth pursuing. Many entry-level positions in the film industry are given to people who have studied liberal arts, cinema, or both.

In the United States there are more than a 1,000 colleges, universities, and trade schools that offer classes in film or television studies; more than 120 of these offer undergraduate programs, and more than 50 grant master's degrees. A small number of Ph.D. programs also exist.

Graduation from a film or television program does not guarantee employment in the industry. Some programs are quite expensive, costing more than $50,000 in tuition alone for three years of study. Others do not have the resources to allow all students to make their own films.

Programs in Los Angeles and New York City, the major centers of the entertainment industry, may provide the best opportunities for making contacts that can be of benefit when seeking employment.

Other Requirements

Producers come from a wide variety of backgrounds. Some start out as magazine editors, business school graduates, actors, or secretaries, messengers, and production assistants for a film studio. Many have never formally studied film.

Most producers, however, get their position through several years of experience in the industry, perseverance, and a keen sense for what projects will be artistically and commercially successful.

Exploring

There are many ways to gain experience in filmmaking. Some high schools have film and video clubs, for example, or courses on the use of motion picture equipment. Experience in high school or college theater can also be useful. One of the best ways to get experience is to volunteer for a student or low-budget film project; positions on such projects are often advertised in local trade publications. Community cable stations also hire volunteers and may even offer internships.

Employers
Many producers in the field are self-employed. Others are salaried employees of film companies, television networks, and television stations. The greatest concentration of motion picture producers is in Hollywood and New York City. Hollywood alone has more than 2,000 producers.

Starting Out
Becoming a producer is similar to becoming president of a company. Unless a person is independently wealthy and can finance whichever projects he or she chooses, prior experience in the field is necessary. Because there are so few positions, even with experience it is extremely difficult to become a successful producer.

Most motion picture producers have attained their position only after years of moving up the industry ladder. Thus, it is important to concentrate on immediate goals, such as getting an entry-level position in a film company. Some enter the field by getting a job as a production assistant. An entry-level production assistant may photocopy copies of the scripts for actors to use, assist in setting up equipment, or may perform other menial tasks, often for very little or even no pay. While a production assistant's work is often tedious and of little seeming reward, it nevertheless does expose one to the intricacies of filmmaking and, more important, creates an opportunity to make contacts with others in the industry.

Those interested in the field should approach film companies, television stations, or the television networks about employment opportunities as a production assistant. Small television stations often provide the best opportunity for those who are interested in television producing. Positions may also be listed in trade publications.

Advancement

There is little room for advancement beyond the position, as producers are at the top of their profession. Advancement for producers is generally measured by the types of projects, increased earnings, and respect in the field. At television stations, a producer can advance to program director. Some producers become directors or make enough money to finance their own projects.

Earnings

Producers are generally paid a percentage of the project's profits or a fee negotiated between the producer and a studio. Average yearly earnings range from about $25,000 to $70,000. The U.S. Department of Labor reports that actors, directors, and producers earned average salaries of $27,400 in 1998. Producers of highly successful films can earn as much as $200,000 or more, while those who make low-budget, documentary films might earn considerably less than the average. In general, producers in the film industry earn more than television producers. A producer for a large market news program can average from about $24,000 to $40,000 a year. Smaller markets pay less, about $17,000 a year. Entry-level production assistants can earn from less than minimum wage to $15,000 per year.

Work Environment

Producers have greater control over their working conditions than most other people working in the motion picture industry. They may have the autonomy of choosing their own projects, setting their own hours, and delegating duties to others as necessary. The work often brings considerable personal satisfaction. But it is not without constraints. Producers must work within a stressful schedule complicated by competing work pressures and often daily crises. Each project brings a significant financial and professional risk. Long hours and weekend work are common. Most producers must provide for their own health insurance and other benefits.

Outlook

Employment for producers is expected to grow faster than the average through the year 2008, according to the U.S. Department of Labor. The occupation of TV news producer was recently listed as a runner-up in *U.S. News & World Report*'s annual compilation of 20 hot track careers. Though opportunities may increase with the expansion of cable television and news programs, video rentals, and an increased overseas demand for American-made films, competition for jobs will be high. Live theater and entertainment will also provide job openings. Some positions will be available as current producers leave the workforce.

TO LEARN MORE ABOUT PRODUCERS

Books

Heath, David. *Television Production Assistant.* Mankato, Minn.: Capstone Press, 1999.

Merbreier, W. Carter. *Television: What's Behind What You See.* New York: Farrar, Straus & Giroux, 1995.

Miller, Marilyn. *Behind the Scenes at the TV News Studio.* Austin: Raintree/Steck-Vaughn, 1996.

Websites

PBS Online

http://www.pbs.org

Provides an overview of the types of educational programs and entertainment aired on public television

Sundance Institute

http://www.sundance.org/index.htm

The official website of the nonprofit organization founded by actor Robert Redford and dedicated to the support and education of new filmmakers

UCLA Department of Film and TV

http://www.tft.ucla.edu/filmtv/ftvba.htm

For information about courses offered in the two-year program in film and television studies and the school's internship program

Where to Write

American Film Institute

2021 North Western Avenue
Los Angeles, CA 90027

Producers Guild of America

400 South Beverly Drive, Suite 211
Beverly Hills, CA 90212

HOW TO BECOME AN ACTOR

The Job

Actors play parts or roles in dramatic productions on the stage, in motion pictures, or on television or radio. They impersonate, or portray, characters by speech, gesture, song, and dance. The imitation of a character for presentation to an audience often seems like a glamorous and easy job. In reality, it is demanding, tiring work requiring special talents.

The actor must first find a part available in some upcoming production. This may be in a comedy, drama, musical, or opera. Then the actor must audition before the director and other people who have control of the production. This requirement is often waived for established artists. In film and television, actors must also complete screen tests, which are scenes recorded on film, at times performed with other actors, which are later viewed by the director and producer of the film.

If selected for the part, the actor must spend hundreds of hours in rehearsal and must memorize many lines and cues. This is especially true in live theater; in film and television, actors may spend less time in rehearsal and sometimes improvise their lines before the camera, often performing several attempts, or "takes," before the director is satisfied. Actors on television often take advantage of teleprompters, which scroll their lines on a screen in front of them while performing. Radio actors generally read from a script, and therefore rehearsal times are usually shorter.

Actors in the theater may perform the same part many times a week for weeks, months, and sometimes years. This allows them to develop the role, but it can also become tedious. Actors in films may spend several weeks involved in a production, which often takes place on location—that is, in different parts of the world. Television actors involved in a series, such as a soap opera or a situation comedy, also may play the same role for years. For these actors, however, their lines change from week to week and even from day to day, and much time is spent rehearsing their new lines.

While studying and perfecting their craft, many actors work as extras, the nonspeaking characters who appear in the background on screen or stage. Many actors also continue their training. A great deal of an actor's time is spent attending auditions.

Requirements

High School There are no minimum educational requirements to become an actor. However, at least a high school diploma is recommended.

Postsecondary As acting becomes more and more involved with the various facets of our society, a college degree will become more important to those who hope to have an acting career. It is assumed that the actor who has completed a liberal arts program is more capable of understanding the wide variety of roles that are available. Therefore, it is strongly recommended that aspiring actors complete at least a bachelor's degree program in theater or the dramatic arts. In addition, graduate degrees in the fine arts or in drama are nearly always required should the individual decide to teach dramatic arts. College can also serve to provide acting experience for the hopeful actor. Actors and directors recommend that those interested in acting gain as much experience as possible through acting in plays in high school and college or in those offered by community groups. Training beyond college is recommended, especially for actors interested in entering the theater. Joining acting workshops, such as the Actors Studio, can often be highly competitive.

Exploring

The best way to explore this career is to participate in school or local theater productions. Even working on the props or lighting crew will provide insight into the field. Also, attend as many dramatic productions as possible and try to talk with people who either are currently in the theater or have been at one time. They can offer advice to individuals interested in a career in the theater.

Employers

Motion pictures, television, and the stage are the largest fields of employment for actors, with television commercials representing as much as 60 percent of all acting jobs. Most of the opportunities for employment in these fields are either in Los Angeles or in New York. On stage, even the road shows often begin in New York, with the selection of actors conducted there along with rehearsals. However, nearly every city and most communities present local and regional theater productions.

The lowest numbers of actors are employed for stage work. In addition to Broadway shows and regional theater, there are employment opportunities for stage actors in summer stock, at resorts, and on cruise ships.

Starting Out

Probably the best way to enter acting is to start with high school, local, or college productions and to gain as much experience as possible on that level. Very rarely is an inexperienced actor given an opportunity to perform on stage or in film in New York or Hollywood. The field is extremely difficult to enter; the more experience and ability beginners have, however, the greater the possibilities for entrance.

Those venturing to New York or Hollywood are encouraged first to have enough money to support themselves during the long waiting and searching period normally required before a job is found. Most will list themselves with a casting agency that will help them find a part as an extra or a bit player, either in theater or film. These agencies keep names on file along with photographs and descriptions of the individuals' features and experience, and if parts comes along that may be suitable, they contact the appropriate people.

Advancement

New actors will normally start in bit parts and will have only a few, if any, lines to speak. The normal procession of advancement would then lead to larger supporting roles and then, in the case of theater, possibly to a role as understudy for one of the main actors. The understudy usually has an opportunity to fill in should the main actor be unable to give a performance. Many film and television actors get their start in commercials or by appearing in government and commercially sponsored public service announcements, films, and programs. Other actors join the afternoon soap operas and continue on to evening programs. Many actors have also gotten their start in on-camera roles such as presenting the weather segment of a local news program. Once an actor has gained experience, he or she may go on to play stronger supporting roles or even leading roles in stage, television, or film productions. From there, an actor may go on to stardom. Only a very small number of actors ever reach that pinnacle, however.

Earnings

The wage scale for actors is largely controlled through bargaining agreements reached by various unions in negotiations with producers. These agreements normally control the minimum salaries, hours of work permitted per week, and other conditions of employment. In addition, each artist enters into a separate contract that may provide for higher salaries.

The 1997 minimum weekly salary for actors in Broadway productions was $1,040, according to the Actors' Equity Association. Minimum salaries for those performing in "Off Broadway" productions ranged from $450 to $600 a week, depending on the size of the theater. Smaller capacity theater productions paid about $400 to $600 weekly. Touring shows paid an additional $100 a day. A steady income is not the norm for most stage actors. Less than 50 percent of those belonging to the Actors' Equity Association found stage work in 1998; average earnings were less than $10,000.

According to the Screen Actors Guild, actors appearing in motion pictures or television shows were paid a daily minimum of $576, or $2,000 a week, in 1998. Extras earned a minimum of $99 a day. Motion picture actors may also receive additional payments known as residuals as part of their guaranteed salary. Many motion picture actors receive residuals whenever films, TV shows, and TV commercials in which they appear are rerun, sold for TV exhibition, or put on videocassette. Residuals often exceed the actors' original salary and account for about one-third of all actors' income.

The annual earnings of persons in television and movies are affected by frequent periods of unemployment. Most guild members earn less than $5,000 a year from acting jobs. Unions offer health, welfare, and pension funds for members working more than a set number of weeks a year. Some actors are eligible for paid vacation and sick time, depending on the work contract.

Work Environment

Actors work under varying conditions. Those employed in motion pictures may work in air-conditioned studios one week and be on location in a hot desert the next.

Those in stage productions perform under all types of

conditions. The number of hours employed per day or week vary, as do the number of weeks employed per year. Stage actors normally perform eight shows per week with any additional performances paid for as over-time. The basic workweek after the show opens is about thirty-six hours unless major changes in the play are needed. The number of hours worked per week is considerably more before the opening, because of rehearsals. Evening work is a natural part of a stage actor's life. Rehearsals often are held at night and over holidays and weekends. If the play goes on the road, much traveling will be involved.

A number of actors cannot receive unemployment compensation when they are waiting for their next part, primarily because they have not worked enough to meet the minimum eligibility requirements for compensation. Sick leaves and paid vacations are not usually available to the actor. However, union actors who earn the minimum qualifications now receive full medical and health insurance under all the actors' unions. Those who earn health plan benefits for ten years become eligible for a pension upon retirement. The acting field is very uncertain. Aspirants never know whether they will be able to get into the profession, and, once in, there are uncertainties as to whether the show will be well received and, if not, whether the actors' talent can survive a bad show.

Outlook

Jobs in acting are expected to grow faster than the average through the year 2008. There are a number of reasons for this. The growth of satellite and cable television in the past decade has created a demand for more actors, especially as the cable networks produce more and more of their own programs and films. The rise of home video has also created new acting jobs, as more and more films are made strictly for the home video market. Many resorts built in the 1980s and 1990s present their own theatrical productions, providing more job opportunities for actors. Jobs in theater, however, face pressure as the cost of mounting a production rises and as many nonprofit and smaller theaters lose their funding.

Despite the growth in opportunities, there are many more actors than there are roles, and this is likely to remain true for years to come. This is true in all areas of the arts, including radio, television, motion pictures, and theater, and even those who are employed are normally employed during only a small portion of the year. Many actors must supplement their income by working as secretaries, waiters, or taxi drivers, for example. Almost all performers are members of more than one union in order to take advantage of various opportunities as they become available.

Of the 105,000 or so actors in the United States today, only about 16,000 are employed at any one time. Of these, few are able to support themselves on their earnings from acting, and fewer still will ever achieve stardom. Most actors work for many years before becoming known, and most of these do not rise above supporting roles. The vast majority of actors, meanwhile, are still looking for the right break. There are many more applicants in all areas than there are positions. As with most careers in the arts, people enter this career out of a love of acting.

TO LEARN MORE ABOUT ACTORS

Books

Mayfield, Katherine. *Young Person's Guide to a Stage or Screen Career.* New York: Watson-Guptill, 1998.

Quinlan, Kathryn A. *Actor.* Mankato, Minn.: Capstone Press, 1998.

Stevens, Chambers. *Magnificent Monologues for Kids.* South Pasadena, Calif.: Sandcastle, 1998.

Websites

Academy of Motion Picture Arts and Sciences
http://www.oscars.org/
Contains a database of Academy-Award-winning actors and films, and provides information about lectures, screenings and other events

Cinema Sites

http://www.cinema-sites.com/

Includes links to news about the film and television industries, listings of guilds and associations, on-line versions of movie scripts, and more

Screen Actors Guild

http://sag.com

Contains information of interest to professional actors and includes a history of the organization and information for young performers

Where to Write

Academy of Motion Picture Arts and Sciences
Academy Foundation
8949 Wilshire Boulevard
Beverly Hills, CA 90211-1972

TO LEARN MORE ABOUT OPRAH WINFREY

Books
Brooks, Philip. *Oprah Winfrey: A Voice for the People.* Danbury, Conn.: Franklin Watts, 1999.

Nicholson, Lois P. *Oprah Winfrey: Talking with America.* Broomall, Penn.: Chelsea House, 1997.

Presnall, Judith Janda. *Oprah Winfrey.* San Diego: Lucent, 1999.

Wooten, Sara McIntosh. *Oprah Winfrey: Talk Show Legend.* Berkeley Heights, N.J.: Enslow, 1999.

Websites
The Hall of Business: Oprah Winfrey

www.achievement.org/autodoc/page/win0pro-1

An American Academy of Achievement site that contains a biography of Oprah and an interview with her

Online with Oprah
http://www.oprah.com
Oprah Winfrey's official website; includes biographical details about her and information about her television show, Oprah's Book Club, Oprah's Angel Network, *O* magazine, and many other projects

Time 100: Oprah Winfrey
http://www.time.com/time/time100/artists/profile/winfrey.html
Contains the biography of Oprah Winfrey by Deborah Tannen that appeared in *Time* magazine's survey of the 100 most influential people of the twentieth century

Interesting Places to Visit
Museum of Broadcast Communications
Chicago Cultural Center
78 East Washington
Chicago, IL 60602
312/346-3278 (312/FINE-ART)

Museum of Television and Radio
25 West 52nd Street
New York, NY 10019
212/621-6600

Museum of Television and Radio
465 North Beverly Drive
Beverly Hills, CA 90210
310/786-1000

Harpo Studios

110 North Carpenter Street
Chicago, IL 60607
The Oprah Winfrey Show is taped before a live audience at Harpo Studios in Chicago. Tickets are available free to those who are age 16 or over by writing to Harpo.

INDEX

125

ABOUT THE AUTHOR

Lucia Raatma received her bachelor's degree in English literature from the University of South Carolina and her master's degree in cinema studies from New York University. Both degrees taught her the power of stories, and very often she feels that the best stories are true ones. She was inspired by Oprah Winfrey's life story—a remarkable example of success in spite of adversity.

Lucia Raatma has written a wide range of books for children and young adults. Her books include *Libraries* and *How Books Are Made* (Children's Press); an eight-book general-safety series and a four-book fire-safety series (Bridgestone Books); fourteen titles in a character education series (Bridgestone Books); and several titles for Compass Point Books. She has also written career biographies of Maya Angelou, Bill Gates, Charles Lindbergh, and Laura Ingalls Wilder for the Ferguson Career Biography series.

When she is not researching or writing, she enjoys going to movies and yoga classes, playing tennis, and spending time with her husband, daughter, and golden retriever.